# STEP-UP
# HISTORY

# War and Change
# Ireland 1918–1924

# Richard McConnell

Evans

Published by Evans Brothers Limited
2A Portman Mansions
Chiltern Street
London W1U 6NR

© Evans Brothers Limited 2007

Produced for Evans Brothers Limited by
White-Thomson Publishing Ltd,
Bridgewater Business Centre,
210 High Street,
Lewes, East Sussex BN7 2NH

Printed in China

Project manager: Sonya Newland

Designer: Robert Walster

Consultant: Brian Malone

British Library Cataloguing in Publication Data

McConnell, Richard

War and change : Ireland 1918-1924. - (Step up
Ireland)

1. Ireland - History - War of Independence,
1919-1921 - Juvenile literature 2. Ireland -
History - Civil War 1922-1923 - Juvenile
literature 3. Ireland - Politics and government -
1910-1921 - Juvenile literature

I. Title
941.5'0921

ISBN-13: 9780237533908

**Picture acknowledgements:**

Corbis: pages 1 (Sean Sexton Collection),
5 (Hulton-Deutsch Collection), 6 (Hulton-Deutsch
Collection), 10 and cover (Bettmann), 11 (Sean
Sexton Collection), 12 (Bettmann), 14 (Hulton-
Deutsch Collection), 15 (Hulton-Deutsch
Collection), 16 (Hulton-Deutsch Collection),
18 (Hulton-Deutsch Collection), 20 (Sean Sexton
Collection), 21 (Bettmann), 22 and cover top left
(Underwood & Underwood), 24 (Hulton-Deutsch
Collection), 25 (Geray Sweeney), 26 (Hulton-
Deutsch Collection), 27 (Paul Seheult; Eye
Ubiquitous); Mary Evans Picture Library: page 9
(Met Police Authority); Courtesy of the National
Library of Ireland: pages 4, 8, 23; Topfoto.co.uk:
pages 7 and cover top right, 13, 19.

Illustrative work by Robert Walster.

# Contents

Ireland in 1918 ....................................................4

Politics in Ireland ................................................6

War of Independence: the Irish side ......................8

War of Independence: the British side ..................10

The Government of Ireland Act ...........................12

Truce and talks ................................................14

The Anglo-Irish Treaty ......................................16

The countdown to civil war ................................18

Rivals: Collins and de Valera .............................20

Civil War: major events ....................................22

Civil War: the legacy ........................................24

The Irish Free State .........................................26

Glossary .........................................................28

For teachers and parents ..................................30

Index .............................................................32

# Ireland in 1918

In 1918 the whole of Ireland was part of the United Kingdom. It was ruled from a parliament in London. Many people in Ireland did not like being ruled by the British government. They wanted Home Rule. This meant having a parliament in Dublin to deal with Irish issues. The people who wanted Home Rule were known as Nationalists. By 1918, most Irish people were tired of waiting for Home Rule. They were starting to demand even greater independence from Britain. Most Nationalists were now calling for a republic. This meant having an independent Ireland, completely separate from Britain.

## The Union with Britain

Not everyone in Ireland wanted to be free of British rule, though. About one quarter of the population did not want either Home Rule or a republic. They were called Unionists because they wanted to keep the union with Britain. Most Unionists lived in the north of the country in the province of Ulster.

Majority Unionist
Belfast

Majority Nationalist
Dublin

ACKVILLE ST. DUBLIN .967. W.L.

◀ *Dublin is now the capital city of the Republic of Ireland. This shows what Dublin looked like at the start of the twentieth century.*

▶ *Tensions between people in Ulster often resulted in violence. Here, Unionists attack Nationalists on their way to work in a shipyard in Belfast.*

## Republics and kingdoms

Many Irish Nationalists wanted a republic. The word comes from two Latin words, 'res' and 'publica', meaning a country belonging to the people, not the king. Britain is a kingdom, with a queen as the head of state. Use the Internet and other resources to list five kingdoms and five republics in the world today.

## About this book

In this book you will find out how the Irish people tried to gain independence from Britain between 1918 and 1924. First came the War of Independence, when different groups in Ireland fought the British and each other. Eventually a treaty was signed that gave Ireland some independence. However, this treaty resulted in the Irish Civil War, because different groups of people in Ireland still could not agree on how the country should be ruled.

# Politics in Ireland

The First World War ended in November 1918 and the British government held a general election in December that year. In Ireland, Sinn Féin, a radical Nationalist party, won most of the votes. To show that they were unhappy with their country being ruled by Britain, the new Sinn Féin members of parliament (MPs) refused to take their seats in parliament. They were determined to win a republic for Ireland.

## Dáil Éireann

On 21 January 1919, a group of 27 Sinn Féin MPs met at the Mansion House in Dublin. They said this meeting was actually a new Irish parliament called Dáil Éireann, which means 'Assembly of Ireland'. At this first meeting they announced that Ireland was now independent. At a later meeting in April they chose who they wanted as leaders in their new government. Éamon de Valera was elected president of the Dáil, Arthur Griffith became vice-president and Michael Collins became minister for finance.

▼ *The men who attended the first Dáil Éireann in a photograph taken in 1919. Michael Collins (left), Arthur Griffith (centre) and Éamon de Valera (right) are sitting in the front row.*

# The IRA

On the very same day as that first meeting took place, the Irish Republican Army (IRA) began a campaign of violence against the Irish police force, the Royal Irish Constabulary (RIC). The IRA was made up of volunteers. These volunteers were extreme Nationalists, who were willing to fight for an Irish republic. Many of them had taken part in the Easter Rising of April 1916, when a group of Nationalists organised a rebellion against British rule in Dublin. The Easter Rising had failed, and several of the rebels had been executed by the British government. This inspired other people to join the group. Although many members of the IRA were also members of Sinn Féin, it was difficult for Sinn Féin to control the IRA. The IRA men worked in small, local groups led by local men who were not under Sinn Féin's control.

## 21 January 1919

Imagine you are a supporter of the Nationalist cause in Ireland and you lived through this busy day in Irish history. Write a diary entry explaining what has taken place and how you feel about what happened. What do you think of the new leaders of Ireland? Do you think that the IRA had reason to attack the Irish police?

▲ The Easter Rising was a rebellion that took place in 1916. Éamon de Valera was already a Nationalist leader, as you can see from this banner used by the Irish Volunteers, a Nationalist group.

# War of Independence: the Irish side

The IRA wanted to force the British out of Ireland. However, they knew that they were not strong enough to defeat the British army in a normal war. Instead they used a form of fighting known as guerrilla warfare. This meant that small groups of IRA men mounted surprise attacks, called ambushes. They would creep up on police patrols and kill them. From January 1919 until July 1921 about 360 policemen were killed using these tactics.

Members of the Royal Irish Constabulary were chosen as targets because they were trying to keep law and order in Ireland. To the IRA, this meant they were supporters of British rule. Most policemen were Catholics and had lived in Ireland all their lives, but they were still seen as enemies by the IRA. Many policemen resigned from their jobs because they were afraid of the IRA. Even the wives and children of RIC men were threatened.

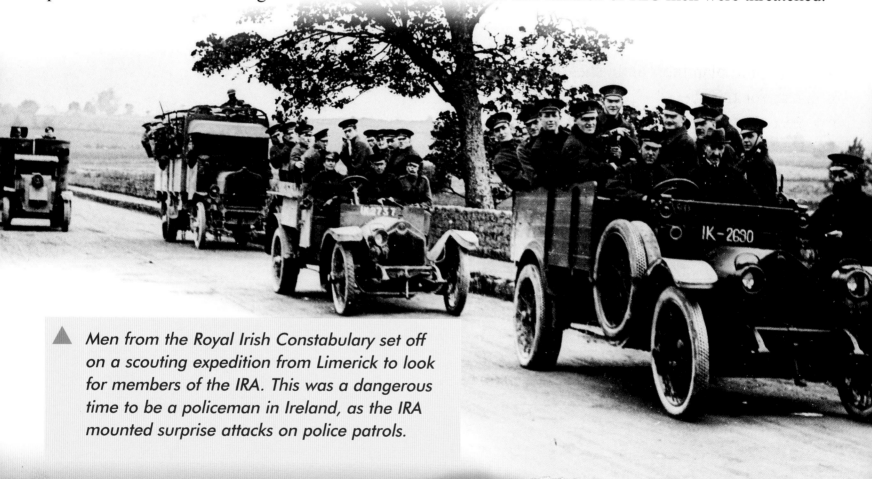

▲ Men from the Royal Irish Constabulary set off on a scouting expedition from Limerick to look for members of the IRA. This was a dangerous time to be a policeman in Ireland, as the IRA mounted surprise attacks on police patrols.

# Flying Columns

As the war continued, the IRA became very skilled at using small, local, well-trained groups of men to carry out ambushes on British soldiers and the RIC. These groups were known as Flying Columns. They worked mainly in the south and south-west of Ireland under local leaders. They would be away from home for months at a time because if they returned home they could easily be caught. They were given food and shelter by Irish people in the countryside who supported them.

It was important that the IRA had good information about police and army patrols so they could plan their ambushes. The Irish minister for finance, Michael Collins, was in charge of getting information from British spies for the IRA. He played a key role in the War of Independence. He was clever and used a secret 'squad' to kill people who were passing information to the British.

## Design a Wanted! poster

General Tom Barry was a guerrilla leader like Daniel Breen. Use the Internet to find out more about him and then design a Wanted! poster for him like the one on this page.

Daniel Breen was an IRA leader in the War of Independence. Who do you think would have offered the reward? What words or phrases in this poster suggest that Daniel Breen is their enemy?

# War of Independence: the British side

The British prime minister at this time was David Lloyd George. Many people in England and America were upset by the growing unrest in Ireland. Lloyd George wanted to find a solution to the problem without having to use the British army. Using the army would have been unpopular in Britain.

Many Irish policemen had resigned or been killed, and most people were too afraid to join the RIC. This meant that there were not enough people in the Irish police force. They desperately needed help to keep order in Ireland. The British government decided to send two groups from England to help the RIC.

## Black and Tans

The first group was nicknamed the 'Black and Tans'. They wore tan-coloured army jackets, with dark RIC trousers because there were not enough proper RIC uniforms to go around. The Black and Tans were young ex-soldiers. They often had very little training, and some showed little discipline.

The IRA started targeting the Black and Tans as well as the RIC. The Black and Tans became angry, as often they could not find the IRA men who had attacked them. They would sometimes round up local people they suspected of being in the IRA, and beat them up or shoot them without a fair trial. On 11 December 1920 the Black and Tans destroyed Cork city centre. Local people began to hate the Black and Tans.

▼ *More than 300 buildings in Cork were set on fire by the Black and Tans.*

IRA guerrilla leader General Tom Barry described how the Black and Tans operated:

*'They had a special technique. Fast lorries of them would come roaring into a village, the occupants would jump out, firing shots and ordering all the inhabitants out of doors. No exceptions were allowed. Men and women, old and young, the sick and the decrepit were lined up against the walls with their hands up, questioned and searched.' (Tom Barry,* Guerrilla Days in Ireland*)*

## The Auxiliaries

The second group sent to help keep order in Ireland were ex-officers who became known as the Auxiliaries. Like the Black and Tans, the Auxiliaries were meant to be part of the RIC, but in rural areas they often worked independently. The Auxiliaries were just as unpopular as the Black and Tans, and became targets for the IRA.

## Taking sides

Draw up a list of the groups who were involved in both sides of the War of Independence. Using the Internet and the information in this book, find out a bit more about each of them. Which group do you think had the most: money; weapons; local knowledge; local support; experience?

|  | IRA | RIC | Auxiliaries |
|---|---|---|---|
| Money |  |  |  |
| Weapons |  |  |  |
| Local knowledge |  |  |  |
| Local support |  |  |  |
| Experience |  |  |  |

# The Government of Ireland Act

In 1920, the British government tried to solve the Irish problem by passing an Act of Parliament. This was called the Government of Ireland Act and it gave Ireland two parliaments. The first was in Dublin and it controlled the southern part of the country. The second was in Belfast and it controlled an area that would be called 'Northern Ireland'. This consisted of six counties of the province of Ulster: Antrim, Armagh, Down, Londonderry, Tyrone and Fermanagh. Of the 1.5 million people living in Northern Ireland in 1920, about one million were Protestant Unionists.

## Too little, too late

The Government of Ireland Act gave Ireland two Home Rule parliaments that would deal with Irish affairs. However, it did not give the country independence. Ireland was still part of the United Kingdom. Sinn Féin and the IRA decided to ignore the Act. It did not give them the republic they had been fighting for. They felt it was too little, too late. Irish politics had moved on and most people wanted more than just Home Rule – they wanted complete independence.

*Crowds in a Dublin street watch as British troops arrest Sinn Féin members, who refused to accept the Government of Ireland Act in 1920.*

# Partition

Even though Sinn Féin tried to ignore it, the Government of Ireland Act was a significant event in Irish history. It divided Ireland into two parts, and a border was created between the six counties of Northern Ireland and the rest of the island. This division is known as partition. The result of this was that the Unionists had their own parliament in Belfast while still being part of the United Kingdom. Although around two-thirds of the people living in the new Northern Ireland were happy with this arrangement, the rest of them (about 500,000) did not like the fact that Ireland had been divided. These people were known as northern Nationalists, and they argued that Ireland should be reunited. Most northern Nationalists were Catholics.

James Craig became the first prime minister of Northern Ireland. The Belfast parliament was officially opened by King George V on 22 June 1921.

## A partition poster

What do you think about the solution offered by the Government of Ireland Act? Design a poster encouraging people to either support or reject the Act. Think of a good slogan. (Hint: use words such as 'partition', 'divided', 'victory' and 'united' as these would provoke a strong reaction.)

This map shows how Ireland was divided by the Government of Ireland Act.

Londonderry

Antrim

Tyrone

Fermanagh

Down

Armagh

# Truce and talks

By the middle of 1921 both sides in the War of Independence wanted a truce. The IRA was running out of weapons and ammunition. The British government was being criticised about some of the actions taken by the Black and Tans. They all wanted to find a compromise and an end to the war.

The president of the Dáil, Éamon de Valera, had been in America, raising support for the Republicans. He returned to Ireland in December 1920. On 11 July 1921, de Valera and Lloyd George decided to call a ceasefire.

## The delegations

They agreed to hold a conference in London to decide how Ireland should be ruled. Lloyd George invited de Valera to send a delegation to represent the Irish. De Valera decided not to go to London himself. Instead he sent a small group led by Michael Collins and Arthur Griffith. Erskine Childers acted as secretary. De Valera told his men not to sign anything before consulting him in Dublin. Their main aims were to achieve a republic for Ireland and to reject the partition of Ireland.

The British delegation was headed by the prime minister, David Lloyd George. He was assisted by Winston Churchill, Austin Chamberlain and Lord Birkenhead. They were determined to keep Ireland within the British Commonwealth.

*The Irish delegation that took part in the treaty talks – Arthur Griffith (third from the right) with other members of Sinn Féin in October 1921.*

# At the negotiating table

Negotiations lasted from October until December 1921. The most important issues being discussed were:

- The relationship between an Irish state and Britain

- Partition

- Britain's access to Irish ports

The British team were very good negotiators, and by December the Irishmen were feeling the pressure. Finally, at 2.10 a.m. on 6 December 1921, the Irish delegates signed the 'Treaty between Great Britain and Ireland'. Under pressure from the British prime minister, Collins and his delegation had not had time to consult with de Valera back in Ireland.

## Chart the differences

Draw up a table to chart the different aims of the two sides during the truce talks. Put the Irish aims on one side and the British aims on the other.

▲ David Lloyd George had threatened that there would be a return to war 'within three days' if the Irish delegation did not sign the Treaty. You can see Michael Collins' signature here (Mícheál Ó Coileáin is the Irish spelling of his name).

# The Anglo-Irish Treaty

On the day he signed the Anglo-Irish Treaty, Michael Collins wrote to a friend, 'Early this morning I signed my death warrant'. He knew that de Valera would not be happy with some of the things his men had agreed to. Here are some of the terms of the Treaty:

- Ireland would be called the Irish Free State

- Ireland would not be a republic. Instead it would be a dominion. This meant that it would be part of the British Commonwealth.

- The king would have a representative in Ireland called the governor-general

- Members of Dáil Éireann and the Irish Senate would take an oath of loyalty to the Irish government and the king of England

- The British navy would still have the use of three Irish ports

- A group called the Boundary Commission would consider the border with Northern Ireland and decide whether or not to give some Nationalist parts of Northern Ireland to the Irish Free State

## Treaty debates

In Ireland, the people could not agree on whether the Treaty was good or bad. They were glad that the war was over, but many, including some leaders of the IRA, were angry that they still did not have a republic. Members of Dáil

▲ *In March 1922, Michael Collins announced the official launch of the Irish Free State to a huge crowd in Dublin. He believed that the Anglo-Irish Treaty offered the country 'The freedom to achieve freedom'. What do you think he meant by that?*

Éireann were on two sides, pro-Treaty (for) and anti-Treaty (against). The anti-Treaty side was led by Éamon de Valera. They still believed in an Irish republic. The pro-Treaty side argued that the Treaty was a big step towards a republic. Michael Collins said that it gave Ireland more independence than the country had ever been offered before. He thought that the only alternative was to go back to a war they would certainly lose.

On 7 January 1922 the Dáil voted on the Treaty. There were 64 votes for it, and 57 against it. The difference of seven votes meant that the Treaty was accepted. As soon as the result was announced, de Valera wept briefly before leading his anti-Treaty supporters from the room.

## In the Dáil

Imagine you were in the Dáil during the discussions about whether or not to accept the Anglo-Irish Treaty. Write a short dialogue between Éamon de Valera and Michael Collins about the advantages and disadvantages. Act this out with a friend.

1916

**April**
*Easter Rising*

**December**
*Sinn Féin MPs refuse to take their seats*

1918

**21 January**
*First meeting of the Dáil. RIC is targeted by IRA.*

1919

**23 December**
*Government of Ireland Act is passed*

**22 June**
*George V opens Northern Ireland Parliament*

1920

**11 July**
*Ceasefire is agreed*

**6 December**
*Anglo-Irish Treaty is signed*

1921

**7 January**
*The Dáil votes for the Treaty*

1922

# The countdown to civil war

This was a time of great uncertainty in Ireland. Despite attempts at a compromise, tension between the two sides continued to grow. Éamon de Valera resigned as president of Dáil Éireann and was replaced by Arthur Griffith. De Valera made many controversial speeches against the Treaty all over Ireland. He said that anti-Treaty supporters 'would have to wade through, perhaps, the blood of some of the members of their government in order to get Irish freedom.' What do you think he meant by this?

## Provisional government

Although de Valera was in no mood for compromise, most ordinary people in Ireland seemed to accept the Treaty. More than 400 local groups announced their support for Michael Collins, Griffith and the new provisional government. This support grew as British troops began to leave Ireland. On 16 January 1922, Dublin Castle – which had been the headquarters of British rule in Ireland – was handed over to Michael Collins.

## Seven minutes late

Michael Collins was late arriving for the handing over of Dublin Castle on 16 January 1922. A British general told him off saying, 'Mr Collins, you are seven minutes late'. Collins is said to have replied, 'You've kept us waiting seven hundred years – you can keep your seven minutes!'

## Collins under pressure

Despite these successes, Collins was under pressure. He had to make sure that the transfer of power went smoothly. The IRA had begun to split. Some stayed loyal to the pro-Treaty side, but others vowed to continue fighting for a republic. Collins was worried that this could lead to a civil war. This would mean fighting against people who had once been his supporters. The anti-Treaty IRA became known as the Irregulars, and many of the pro-Treaty IRA members joined the new Irish Free State Army.

On 13 April 1922, anti-Treaty forces attacked the Four Courts building in Dublin and took it over. This was the first step towards war.

## June 1922

It was the events of June 1922 that finally brought Ireland into civil war. A general election was held, and this showed that most of the Irish people supported the Treaty. However, anti-Treaty forces still controlled the Four Courts, and the British government was putting even more pressure on Michael Collins to take a stand against the rebels. On 27 June, a general in the Free State Army was kidnapped by the Irregulars. Collins realised he could not wait any longer. He decided to attack the Four Courts.

▼ *The attack on the Four Courts in Dublin was the first action of the Irish Civil War.*

# Rivals: Collins and de Valera

## 'The Big Fellow' – Michael Collins

Michael Collins was born in Clonakilty, Co. Cork on 18 October 1890. When he was 16 he moved to London to work at the Post Office Savings Bank. During his time there, he worked with other Irish people who had moved to England to find jobs. He joined the Irish Republican Brotherhood in 1909. The IRB was a secret society, determined to find a way of winning a republic for Ireland, even if this meant using violence.

When Collins returned to Ireland in 1916, he became involved in the unsuccessful Easter Rising. Two years later he was elected Sinn Féin MP for South Cork in the general election. He became minister for finance when the new Dáil Éireann met in 1919. During the War of Independence it was Michael Collins who was in charge of getting information from British spies for the IRA (see page 9).

Collins was a good organiser and a practical man. When he was killed in August 1922 (see page 23), the pro-Treaty side lost one of its most able leaders.

▲ Michael Collins, who learned about the Irish Republican Brotherhood while he was still at school – his schoolmaster was a member of the group.

# 'The Long Fellow' – Éamon de Valera

Éamon de Valera was born in Brooklyn, New York in 1882 to Spanish-Irish parents. He grew up in Co. Limerick, and became a teacher. He took part in the Easter Rising, but avoided execution because he was an American citizen. In 1916 Britain hoped that the Americans would join the First World War on their side. Executing an American might have damaged their relations with the United States. De Valera was put in prison in Britain.

He returned to Ireland in 1918. He became the first president of Dáil Éireann. De Valera was an eccentric and solitary character. He did not attend the negotiations in London in 1921, and rejected the Treaty when it was signed by Collins. Some historians think he deliberately sent Collins to London because he knew that the delegation would not win a republic. This way Collins would be forced to take the blame. When de Valera left the Dáil chamber after the Treaty was accepted in 1922, he refused to return until 1927.

◄ Éamon de Valera – photographed here towering over Arthur Griffith. You can see from the pictures on these pages why Collins and de Valera were nicknamed 'The Big Fellow' and 'The Long Fellow'.

## Create a CV

Choose either Michael Collins or Éamon de Valera and write a CV of their achievements. Include sections on personal information (name and date of birth), political career, and talents (the things they were good at). Use the websites listed below to learn more about them if necessary.

- http://www2.cruzio.com/~sbarrett/mcollins.htm
- http://www.historylearningsite.co.uk/eamonn_de_valera.htm

# Civil War: major events

Less than two weeks after the start of its attack on the Four Courts, the provisional government had defeated the Irregulars in Dublin. There was no doubt that the Free State Army was the stronger force. Although they had very little experience, they had weapons and ammunition supplied by the British. They were much better armed than the Irregulars. Soldiers who had once fought together against the British now found themselves on opposite sides. Families were divided. Friend fought against former friend.

## Headline news

The newspaper headlines from the time record the successes of the Free State Army throughout the summer of 1922. These are taken from the *Freeman's Journal*, a popular newspaper at the time. Much of the press was censored during the Civil War. Do you think that these headlines are fully reliable?

■ 'Fall of Limerick: Powerful night assault compels the Irregulars to retreat' (22 July 1922)

■ 'March into County Kerry: The capture of Tralee, Tarbert and Ballylongford taken: advance on Listowel' (5 August 1922)

◄ *Soldiers of the Irish Free State Army keep a lookout for Irregulars. By the end of August 1922, the pro-Treaty side was once more in control of all the major towns and cities in Ireland. The Irregulars resorted to guerrilla warfare, but they had little success, and by December 1922 they were nearly defeated.*

# The death of Michael Collins

On 22 August 1922 Michael Collins was shot dead in an ambush at Béal na mBláth in Co. Cork. Arthur Griffith had died of a brain haemorrhage just 10 days earlier. The provisional government found itself without two of its most able leaders. William T. Cosgrave became the new leader of the Free State government.

The government was determined to put a stop to any rebellions, and decided to come down hard on the IRA. It said that anyone found with a weapon would be executed.

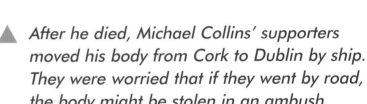

After he died, Michael Collins' supporters moved his body from Cork to Dublin by ship. They were worried that if they went by road, the body might be stolen in an ambush.

## Erskine Childers

Erskine Childers was one of the Irish Treaty delegation that had gone to London. On 24 November 1922, he was executed. Use published or ICT resources to help you write an obituary of Erskine Childers. Remember to include his good points as well as his bad points. You will need to use several sources to get a balance of opinions.

## Sentenced to death

On 7 December 1922, two pro-Treaty Dáil members were shot dead by the Irregulars. The next day four Irregulars were executed. The government wanted to show the Irregulars that they would not stand any more attacks. The anti-Treaty forces were demoralised by the executions.

# Civil War: the legacy

Liam Lynch was the chief of staff of the Irregulars. He was the key leader of the anti-Treaty side and kept the fight going even when it was clear that the pro-Treaty side was winning. When he was killed in April 1923, a ceasefire was finally called.

## The cost of war

It is difficult to know how many people died during the Civil War as detailed records were not made. Estimates range between 1,000 and 4,000 deaths. Of these, 77 were executed by the government under the emergency laws.

The bitterness caused by the war lasted for generations. Families were split over the Treaty. The war came between friends and work colleagues. As well as this bitterness, many of Ireland's big houses were burnt down during the war. Valuable collections of books were lost, as well as paintings and furnishings. The destruction of roads, railways and bridges cost the state dearly and caused problems for the new government.

For 50 years, most of Ireland's politicians could claim to have played some part in the Civil War. The two largest parties in Ireland, Fine Gael and Fianna Fáil, are descended from the pro-Treaty and anti-Treaty sides of the conflict. In this way the Civil War cast a long shadow over Irish politics.

◄ *These people are staging a protest against the execution of members of the Irregulars by the government during the emergency laws.*

Fianna Fáil (which means 'Soldiers of Destiny') is the largest political party in Ireland today. It is descended from the anti-Treaty group of the early 1920s.

## National archives

One of the most serious losses of the Irish Civil War was that of the historical records contained in the Public Record Office at the Four Courts in Dublin. During the attack on the Four Courts in June 1922 almost all the records acquired by the office were destroyed by fire. Many of these important papers dated back to the thirteenth century. Although many have been replaced by copies, others – such as some of the earliest census reports – were lost forever.

16 January 1922 Dublin Castle is handed over to Michael Collins by the British.

13 April 1922 Anti-Treaty forces attack the Four Courts in Dublin.

28 June 1922 Michael Collins orders an attack on the rebels in the Four Courts.

21 July 1922 The city of Limerick falls to the Free State Army.

22 August 1922 Michael Collins is killed in an ambush.

24 November 1922 Erskine Childers is executed.

10 April 1923 Liam Lynch is killed in an attack by the Free State Army.

24 May 1923 The IRA orders its men to give up their weapons to honour the ceasefire.

# The Irish Free State

After the Civil War, William T. Cosgrave started a new pro-Treaty party called Cumann na nGaedhael ('Party of the Irish'). It had a lot of work to do to establish the new state. The southern part of Ireland now had independence from Britain and was known as the Irish Free State. However, the damage caused by the fighting had been very costly. Many people still had guns, and robberies in the countryside were common.

▲ William T. Cosgrave, the first leader of the new Irish Free State.

## New laws

There was a growing need for a new police force to replace the old RIC. To meet this need, the new Irish government set up the Garda Síochána ('Guardians of the Peace'). It also put in place a new court system and made plans to reduce the size of the Free State Army, which had been large so it could cope with the Civil War. Dáil Éireann passed a law called the Public Safety Act to give the government extra powers so it could deal with troublemakers. Despite some setbacks, the government made good progress in building the new state.

## Britain and the Free State

Ireland's relationship with Britain was an important issue. Cosgrave's government wanted to make sure that the Irish Free State was seen as an independent country. From 1924, Irish people used their own Irish passports instead of British passports. The United States recognised Ireland as a separate country from Britain for the first time. Cosgrave was a good leader. He hoped that his careful policies would help Ireland become stable.

> *Sinn Féin still exists today as a Nationalist party. Its members still want complete freedom from British rule in Ireland.*

Another challenge for the new state was helping the economy grow. Farming employed most people in Ireland in the 1920s, so the government focused on making sure that the produce from the farms was of a high standard. This would help Irish farmers get better prices for their eggs, meat and milk. Other successes were the setting up of the Electricity Supply Board (ESB) and using the river Shannon to generate hydroelectric power. The Irish Sugar Company was started in 1926.

## Ireland after the Civil War

Draw a large map of Ireland using the one on page 13 as a reference. Pencil in the border with Northern Ireland. Inside the map write a list of challenges facing the new Irish Free State. In a different colour, write in the successes of Cosgrave's government. Use websites such as the following to help you find out more about the problems facing Ireland after the Civil War: http://www.bbc.co.uk/dna/h2g2/A17719103

## Northern Ireland

1n 1924, partition was still an important issue for many people. Ireland had two governments and two separate parts. Although most Irish people wanted to reunite north and south, there was a majority of Unionists in the north who were content to keep the border and stay part of the United Kingdom. The Boundary Commission (which was set up to redraw the border) failed, and Ireland remained an island with two separate states.

# Glossary

**Act of Parliament** — a law made by the government, which is debated in parliament before being voted for by members of parliament.

**ambushes** — surprise attacks.

**ammunition** — bullets, missiles, grenades and other substances used as weapons.

**anti-Treaty** — those who were against the Anglo-Irish Treaty of 1921.

**archives** — historical records such as government papers, letters and census reports.

**Boundary Commission** — the group that was set up to look at the border between Northern Ireland and the Irish Free State, to decide whether or not to give some of the Nationalist parts of Northern Ireland to the Free State.

**Catholics** — followers of a form of Christianity that believes in the traditions and teachings of the Roman Catholic Church and the authority of the Pope, as well as the Bible.

**ceasefire** — an agreement to stop fighting.

**censored** — when a piece of writing or film is checked and anything considered a threat or offensive is taken out.

**census** — a count of the population.

**civil war** — war between people of the same country.

**Commonwealth** — the countries associated with Britain.

**compromise** — efforts to reach an agreement that take into consideration the views of both sides of an argument.

**consulting** — asking someone's advice.

**controversial** — something that can make people disagree strongly.

**Dáil Éireann** — Assembly of Ireland. The Irish name for the parliament set up in 1919.

**delegation** — a group that represents someone or something.

**demoralised** — discouraged and downhearted about something.

**discipline** — when rules and orders are followed without questioning.

**dominion** — part of a country that rules itself.

**Easter Rising** — a military rebellion organised by some extreme Nationalists in April 1916 to win independence for Ireland. It failed, but it later inspired many people to fight for Irish independence.

**eccentric** — someone who is unusual and does things in a way that is different from most people.

**executed** — put to death as punishment for a crime.

**Fianna Fáil** — 'Soldiers of Destiny'. The anti-Treaty party set up by Éamon de Valera in 1927.

**Fine Gael** 'Family of the Irish'. The pro-Treaty party Cumann na nGaedhael joined with other groups to become known as Fine Gael in 1933.

**Flying Columns** groups of rebels who trained together before attacking other groups in the War of Independence.

**general election** election involving the whole country.

**guerrilla warfare** a type of warfare in which small groups of soldiers carry out surprise attacks on their enemies.

**Home Rule** having a parliament 'at home' in Dublin to rule Irish affairs.

**Irish Republican Brotherhood (IRB)** a secret society that made promises to fight for an Irish republic.

**Irregulars** IRA members who rejected the Anglo-Irish Treaty.

**Nationalists** People who wanted Ireland to rule itself from a parliament in Dublin, rather than being controlled by Britain.

**negotiations** discussions about an issue in an effort to find a solution.

**oath of loyalty** a promise to be loyal and support someone or something.

**obituary** a short article about the life of someone who has died.

**parliament** a meeting of important people from all over the country, to pass laws and provide money for the king or queen

**partition** the division of Ireland into two states with a border between them.

**ports** places where ships load and unload cargo.

**Protestants** followers of a form of Christianity that rejects the teaching of the Roman Church and believes in the Bible as the only authority for Christians.

**pro-Treaty** those people who supported the Anglo-Irish Treaty of 1921.

**province** a part of Ireland. There are four provinces: Ulster, Munster, Leinster and Connacht.

**provisional government** a government that is formed temporarily in times of trouble until a permanent government can be set up.

**rebellion** an act of defiance against the authorities.

**republic** a country belonging to the people, not a king or queen.

**resigned** left their jobs, decided not to work for the police anymore.

**rural** relating to the countryside.

**solitary** preferring to work alone.

**tactics** decisions about how to fight a war.

**truce** an agreement to stop fighting.

**Unionists** People in Ireland who wanted to keep the union with Britain.

**warrant** a document that makes certain that something will happen.

# For teachers and parents

This book is a resource to help children grasp some of the key themes in Irish history between 1918 and 1924. It is particularly suited to children in 4th–6th Class or P5–P7. It fits in with the new Primary Curriculum (Republic of Ireland) Strand: Politics, conflict and society, Strand Unit 1916 and the foundations of the state. This book will also be a useful resource for Key Stage 2 (Northern Ireland) History Strand 3: Our world. In addition, the activities and content of the book would be ideal for Key Stage 2 History in the English National Curriculum under the British History section (aspects of the histories of England, Ireland, Scotland and Wales).

In this book there is a focus on activities that stimulate the different learning styles of children. It is hoped that this book will promote research rather than act as a final text for the period.

Although the activities are designed to develop the skills of the historian, there are links with many other curriculum subjects such as drama, English, geography and art. Children are encouraged to use ICT to assist them in their research where appropriate. There are also opportunities to develop skills of compromise and teamwork, as children are encouraged to consider arguments from more than one side.

The period 1918–1924 was a volatile one in Irish history. There was change and conflict, compromise and obstinacy, high drama and terrible tragedy. The Irish question has proven to be one of the most difficult issues to resolve, and the mistakes of the past are often replayed in the modern political arena. It is difficult to assess the events of the period with detachment. Children must learn to look at all the evidence with caution. They should be encouraged to understand the emotional and cultural issues behind the sources.

## SUGGESTED FURTHER ACTIVITIES

### Pages 4–5 Ireland in 1918

Irish history did not begin in 1918. The Easter Rising of April 1916 provoked controversy and inspired many Irish people with Republican ideals. Children could research this rebellion and try to understand how the British response rather than its military success was the catalyst to the Republican movement.

Children could find out more about the Home Rule crisis of 1912–1914 and how the Unionists tried to prevent Home Rule before the outbreak of the First World War in 1914. Suitable topics for exploration are the Ulster Solemn League and Covenant of September 1912 and the Ulster Volunteer Force, 1913.

### Pages 6–7 Politics in Ireland

Children could look at the results of the 1910 general elections and compare them with the 1918 general elections. This would show them the extent of the Sinn Féin landslide.

Children could compare and contrast the aims of the Sinn Féin party that was founded in 1905 by Arthur Griffith with the Sinn Féin that sat in the first Dáil Éireann. They were very different.

### Pages 8–9 War of Independence: the Irish side

There are pictures of Flying Columns available on the Internet. It would be an interesting exercise for the children to look at these old group photographs and describe the appearance of the IRA men and the weapons they had.

The RIC was a troubled organisation by 1919. Children could look at the badges of the organisation and try to find out what the different symbols stood for.
http://www.psni.police.uk/index/pg_police_museum/pg_the_royal_irish_constabulary.htm.

### Pages 10–11 War of Independence: the British side

The Black and Tans and Auxiliaries are good topics for further research. Using pictures from books or the Internet, children could describe their appearance. They could try to explain why they were so hated by the local population.

Children living in Ireland can check local libraries and museums for artefacts and pictures of the Black and Tans and Auxiliaries. There are some excellent examples of artefacts and photographs on:
http://www.clarelibrary.ie/eolas/claremuseum/projects/war_of_independence_collection.htm.

Children could write up a CV for David Lloyd George. They could consider his personal impact on the Irish question.

### Pages 12–13 The Government of Ireland Act

The topic of partition always provokes lively debate. The alternatives to a six-county Northern Ireland were explored during the Home Rule Crisis and at the Buckingham Palace Conference of 1914. Children could explore the pros and cons for Unionists (and Nationalists) of a four, six or nine-county partition.

Children could consider the strengths and weaknesses of the Government of Ireland Act as a solution to the Irish question, and prepare speeches either supporting or rejecting the Act/Partition.

Children could look at the settlement of Protestants in Ulster. The BBC history site is: http://www.bbc.co.uk/history/british/plantation/index.shtml.

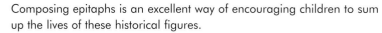

### Pages 14–15 Truce and talks

This aspect of the period is especially suited to drama and re-enactment. After studying the negotiations, a group of children could play the roles of the British and Irish delegates at the Treaty negotiations. They could first draw up a script before acting out the final stages of the negotiations and finish with the signing of the Treaty.

The Irish delegates signed the Treaty using their Irish names. This would be an excellent opportunity for children to learn to write Irish versions of their own names or those of the Irish delegates.

### Pages 16–17 The Anglo-Irish Treaty

The Anglo-Irish Treaty became one of the most divisive documents in modern Irish history. Children could study a simplified version of its terms and add or remove any of the terms as part of a 'Treaty Amendment' exercise. A group of children could suggest alternative terms or changes before voting on them as a class.

Children could consider the pros and cons of the Treaty and try to understand why Collins and Griffith signed it and why de Valera was so adamantly against it.

### Pages 18–19 The countdown to civil war

It was six months between the signing of the Treaty and the outbreak of war. Children may like to do some further research on this unsettled period and prepare a timeline of the major events.

There were some interesting clashes of personality during this period, the most fascinating being Collins/de Valera. Children could write a diary entry of Collins/de Valera about the other leader. Collins died in an ambush in August 1922. It could be an interesting exercise to write the private and public reactions of de Valera to the incident.

### Pages 20–21 Rivals: Collins and de Valera

Children may want to compile a photo album of both/one of these leaders. See http://www.generalmichaelcollins.com/ for an excellent selection of photographs from Collins' life.

The children could consider the difference in the personalities and leadership styles of both men and decide who was the best leader/politician. De Valera died in 1975 after a long career in politics. Children could research his life and career after 1924.

### Pages 22–23 Civil War: major events

Many famous Irish men died during the Civil War. An activity compiling a collection of obituaries of some of these figures – Collins, Griffith, Childers, Rory O'Connor, Liam Lynch – would be a good exercise.

Composing epitaphs is an excellent way of encouraging children to sum up the lives of these historical figures.

### Pages 24–25 Civil War: the legacy

The Civil War was a watershed in Irish history. Children could be encouraged to trace the development of either Fine Gael or Fianna Fáil from its Civil War roots.

The loss of the archives in the Public Record Office could lead to an interesting discussion about the importance of looking after our heritage and storing our historical documents safely. Students could make a list of different kinds of sources and talk about how archives help us preserve our history for future generations.

### Pages 26–27 The Irish Free State

Children could research the period between 1924 and the establishment of the Republic of Ireland in 1949. They could draw a timeline to show the main events of the period and look at the lives and careers of the leaders of independent Ireland.

## BOOKS AND WEBSITES

There are very few books available that deal with this period specifically. One book that gives a good background is *The Guns of Easter* by Gerard Whelan (O'Brien Press). The following websites are an excellent starting point for research in this area:

For Unionism, the Public Record Office of Northern Ireland has an excellent resource on the Ulster Covenant at: http://www.proni.gov.uk/ulstercovenant/index.html

There is some old film footage available of the Easter Rising and the War of Independence on: http://www.learningcurve.gov.uk/onfilm/empire.htm

The BBC website is well-written and accessible, if a little advanced for younger children: http://www.bbc.co.uk/history/british/easterrising/

Black and Tans: http://www.historylearningsite.co.uk/black_and_tans.htm

For children interested in finding out more about Northern Ireland the following site is good: http://www.bbc.co.uk/history/recent/troubles/index.shtml

These websites contain some extra biographical material:

Michael Collins biography: http://www2.cruzio.com/~sbarrett/mcollins.htm

http://www.schoolsat.net/teachers/act_loc_hist/michael_collins.pdf

De Valera: http://www.historylearningsite.co.uk/eamonn_de_valera.htm

A timeline for Irish history of the twentieth century is available at http://www.teachnet.ie/dhorgan/index.html

# Index

ambushes  8, 9, 23, 25
America  10, 14, 21, 26
Anglo-Irish Treaty  5, 15,
  16–17, 18, 21, 24
Antrim  12, 13
archives  25
Armagh  12, 13
Auxiliaries  11

Barry, General Tom  9, 11
Béal na mBláth  23
Belfast  4, 5, 12, 13
Birkenhead, Lord  14
Black and Tans  10, 11, 14
Boundary Commission
  16, 27
Breen, Daniel  9
Britain  4, 5, 6, 15, 21, 26
British army  8, 10
British government  4, 6,
  7, 8, 12, 14, 19

Catholics  8, 13
Chamberlain, Austin  14
Childers, Erskine  14, 23,
  25
Churchill, Winston  14
Civil War  5, 18, 19,
  22–23, 24–25, 26, 27
Collins, Michael  6, 9, 14,
  15, 16, 17, 18, 19, 20,
  21, 23, 25
Commonwealth  14, 16

Cork  10, 20, 23
Cosgrave, William T.  23,
  26, 27
Craig, James  13
Cumann na nGaedhael
  26

Dáil Éireann  6, 14, 16,
  17, 18, 20, 21, 23, 26
de Valera, Éamon  6, 7,
  14, 15, 16, 17, 18, 21
Down  12, 13
Dublin  4, 6, 7, 12, 14,
  16, 19, 22, 23, 25
Dublin Castle  18, 25

Easter Rising  7, 17, 20, 21
Electricity Supply Board  27

farming  27
Fermanagh  12, 13
Fianna Fáil  24, 25
Fine Gael  24
First World War  6, 21
Flying Columns  9
Four Courts  19, 22, 25
Free State Army  19, 22,
  25, 26
Freeman's Journal  22

Garda Síochána  26
George, David Lloyd  10,
  14, 15

Government of Ireland Act
  12, 13, 17
Griffith, Arthur  6, 14, 18,
  21, 23
guerrilla warfare  8, 22

Home Rule  4, 12

independence  4, 5, 6, 12,
  17, 26
IRA (Irish Republican Army)
  7, 8, 9, 10, 11, 12, 14,
  16, 17, 19, 20, 23, 25
IRB (Irish Republican
  Brotherhood)  20
Irish Free State  16, 26–27
Irish Sugar Company  27
Irregulars  19, 22, 23, 24

Limerick  8, 22, 25
London  4, 14, 20, 21, 23
Londonderry  12, 13
Lynch, Liam  24, 25

Nationalists  4, 5, 6, 7,
  13, 16
Northern Ireland  12, 13,
  16, 27

oath of loyalty  16

parliament  4, 12, 13, 17
partition  13, 15, 27

Protestants  12
provisional government
  18, 22, 23

republic  4, 5, 6, 7, 12,
  16, 17, 19, 20, 21
RIC (Royal Irish
  Constabulary)  7, 8, 9,
  10, 11, 17, 26

Shannon, river  27
Sinn Féin  6, 7, 12, 13,
  14, 17, 20
spies  9, 20

Tyrone  12, 13

Ulster  4, 5, 12
Unionists  4, 5, 12, 13, 27
United Kingdom  4, 12,
  13, 27

War of Independence
  5, 8–9, 10–11, 14, 20
weapons  11, 14, 22,
  23, 26